TABLE OF CONTENTS

Good King Wenceslas

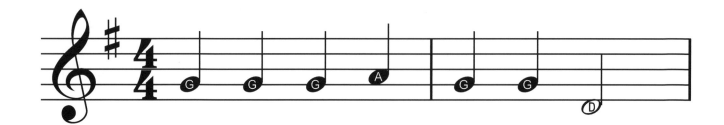

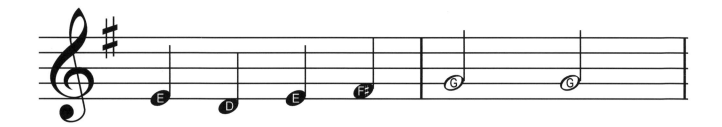

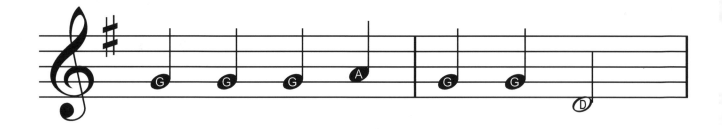

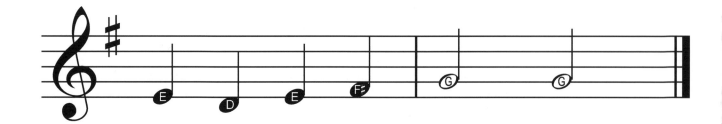

Hot Cross Buns

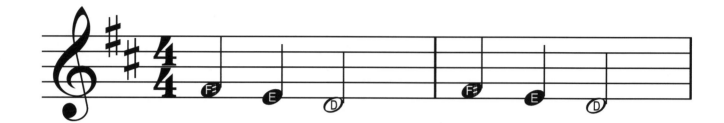

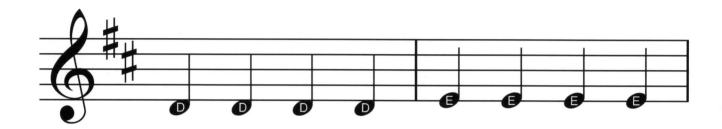

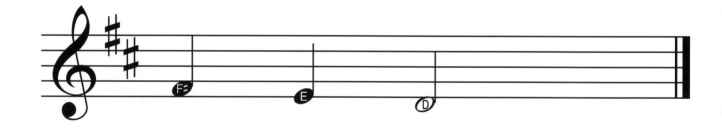

Mary Had a Little Lamb

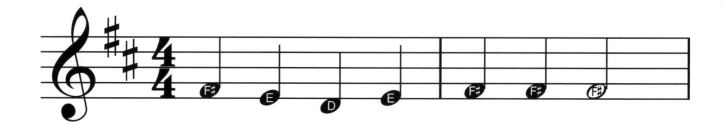

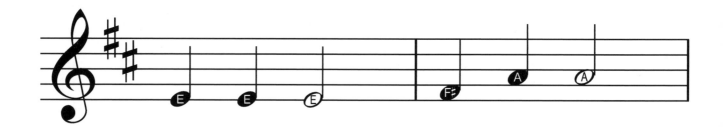

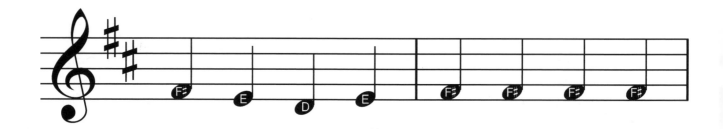

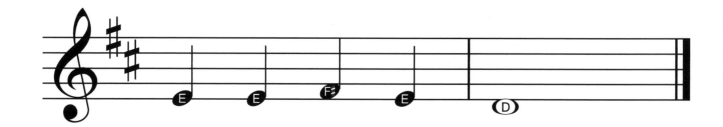

Lightly Row

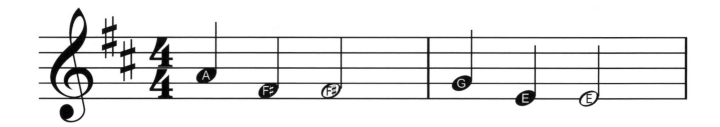

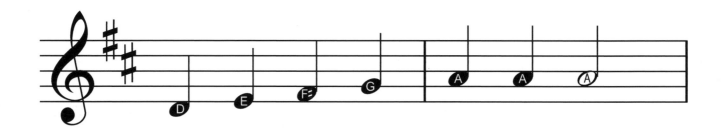

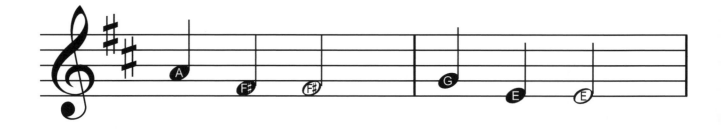

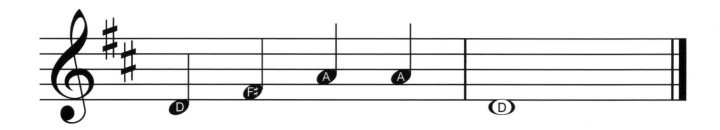

Aura Lee

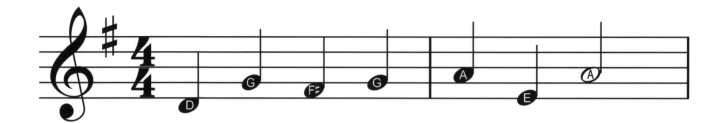

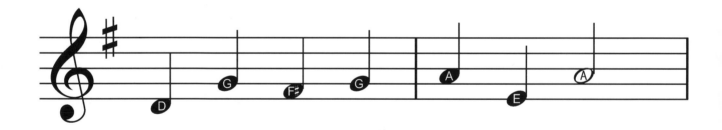

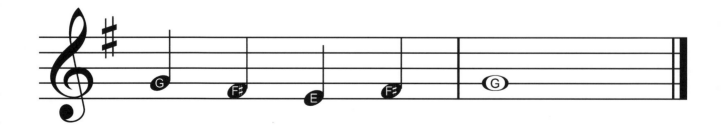

Go Tell Aunt Rhody

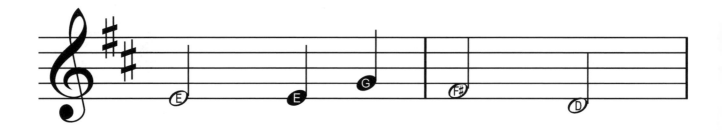

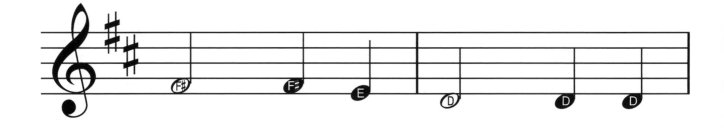

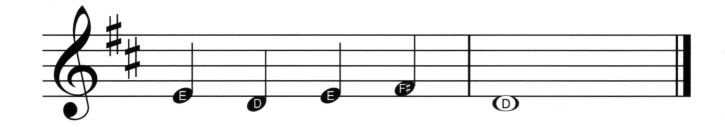

Frog Song

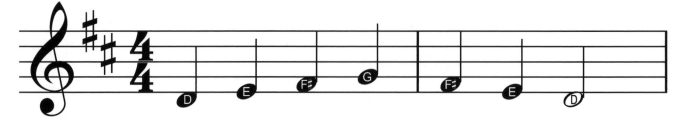

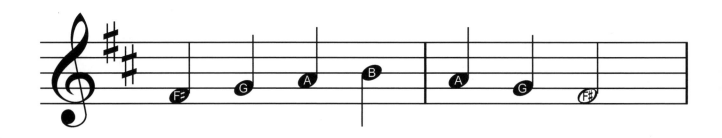

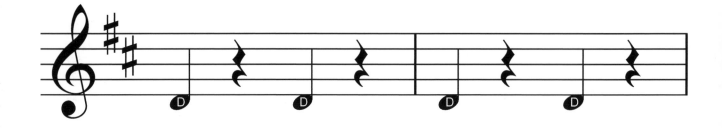

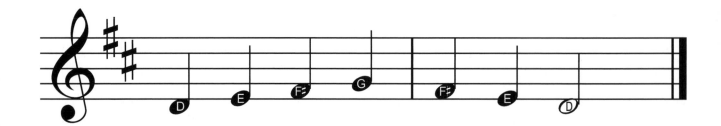

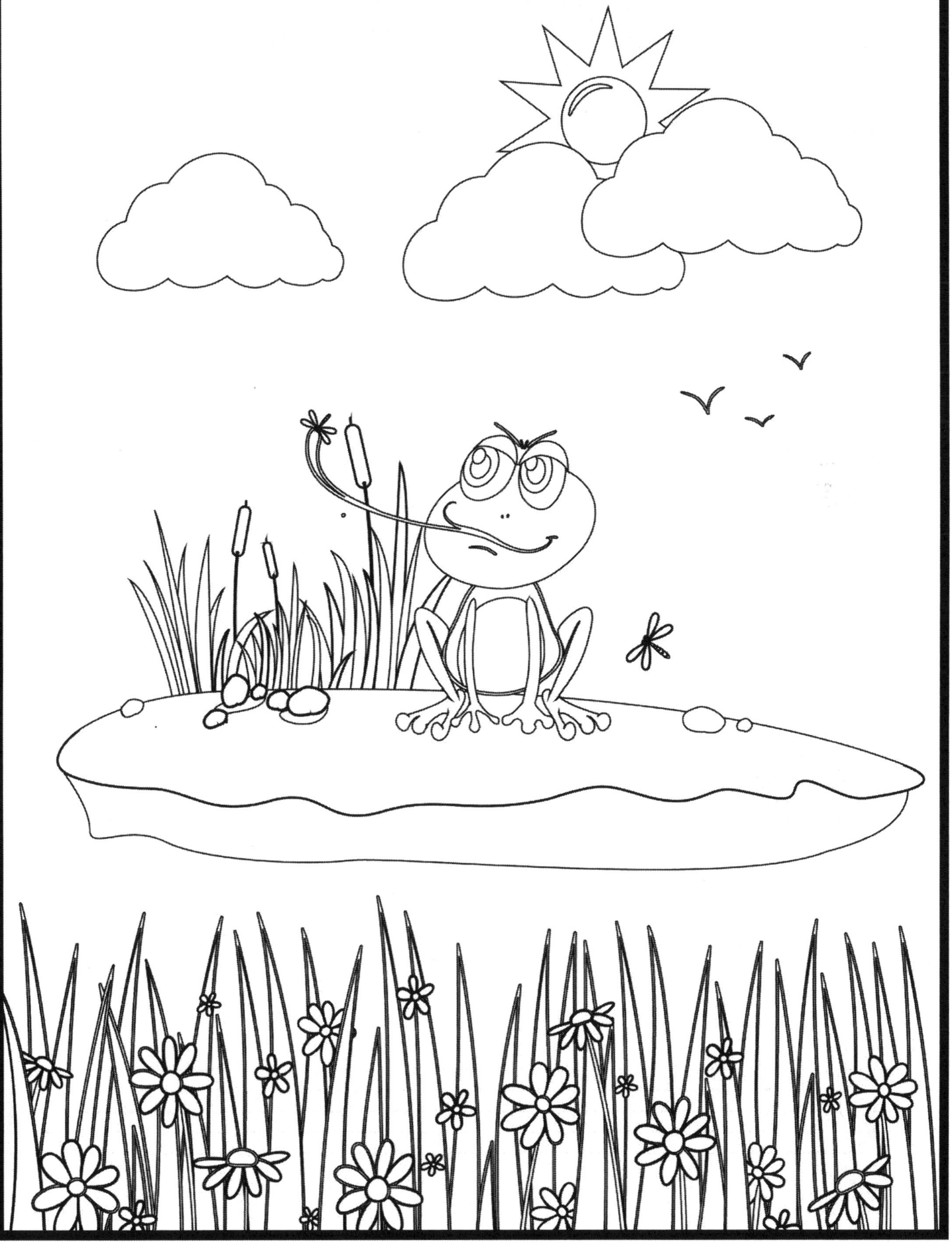

Camptown Races

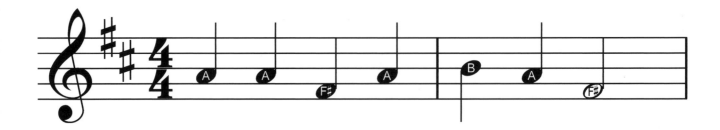

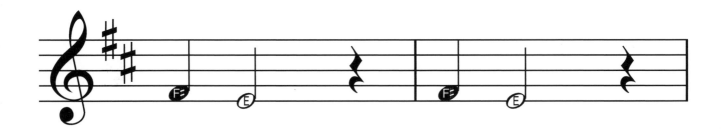

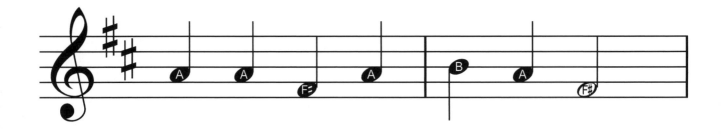

London Bridge

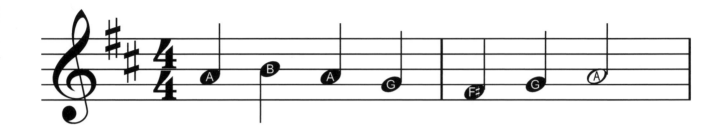

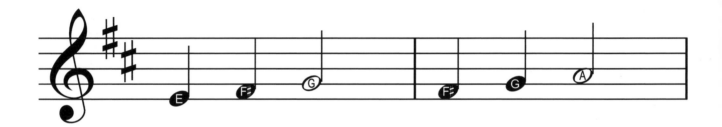

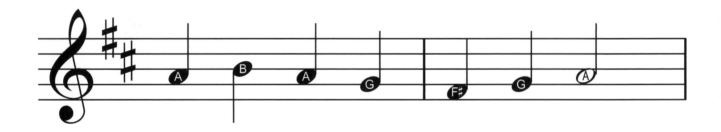

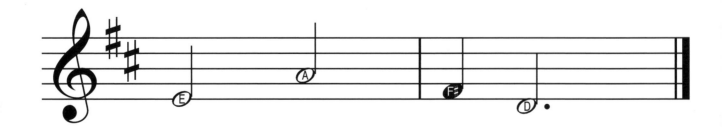

Dreydl, Dreydl

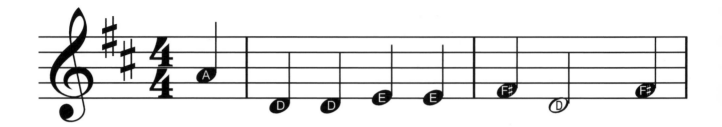

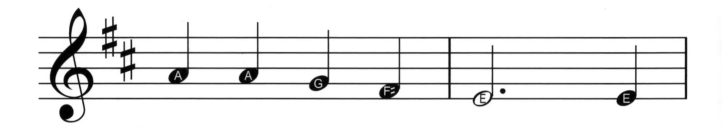

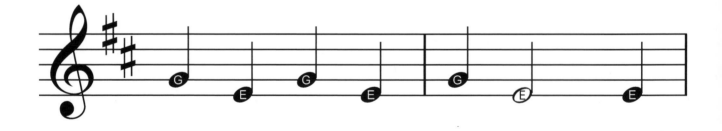

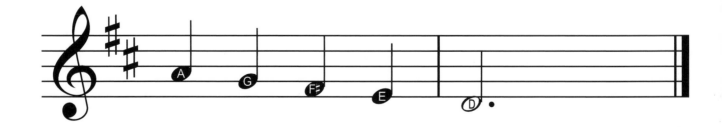

Twinkle, Twinkle, Little Star

Jolly Old St. Nicholas

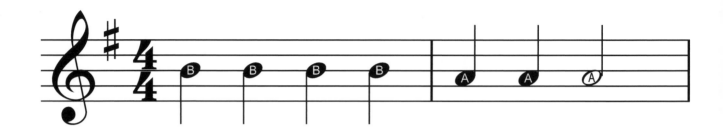

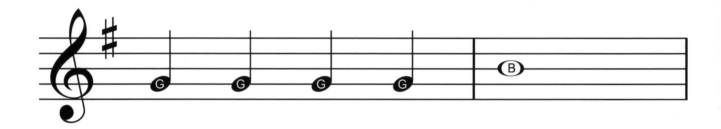

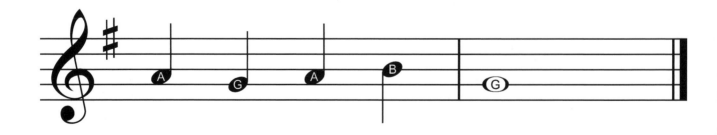

The Bridge at Avignon

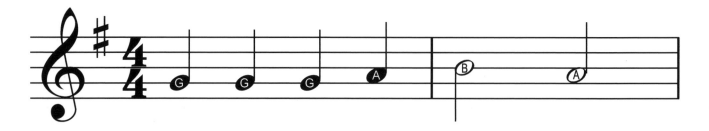

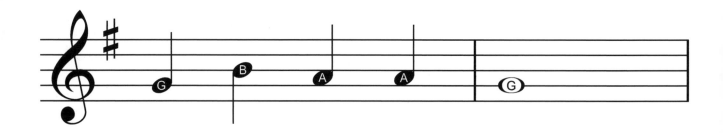

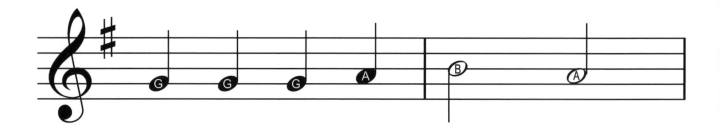

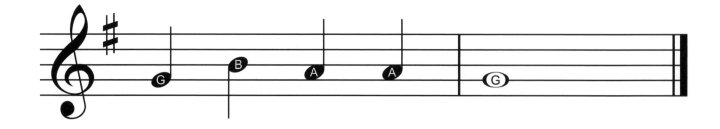

Pop Goes the Weasel

Jingle Bells

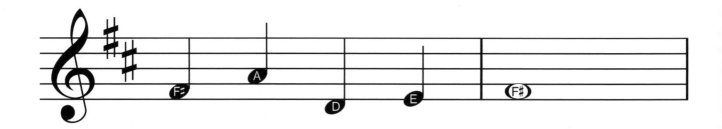

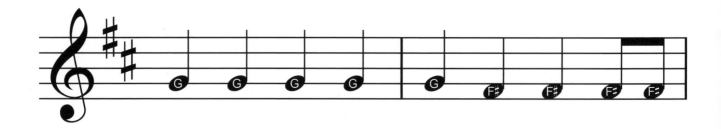

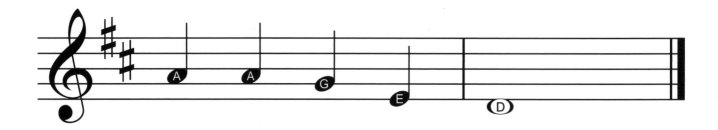

Are You Sleeping?

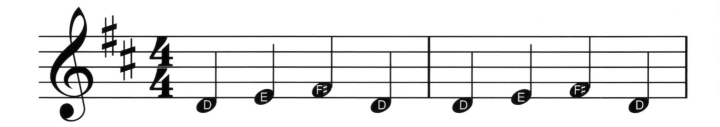

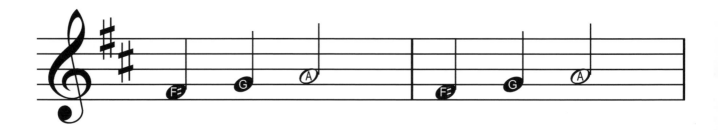

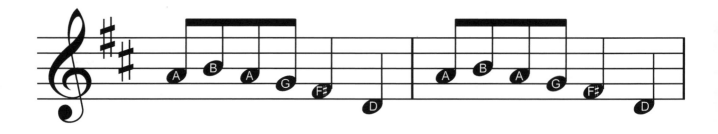

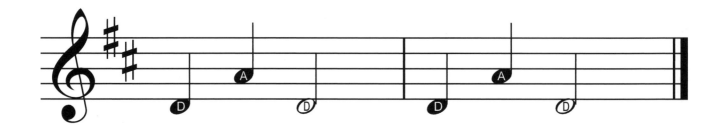

Musette

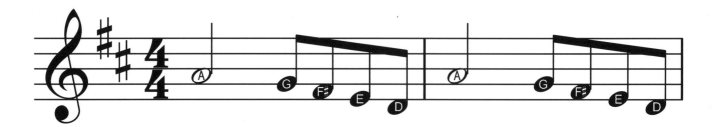

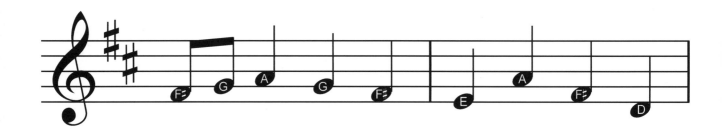

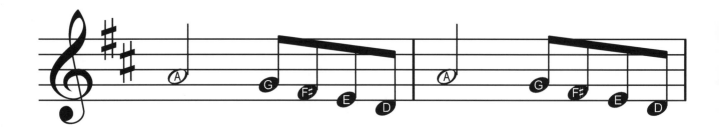

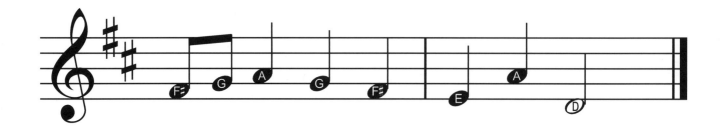

Lo Yisa Goy

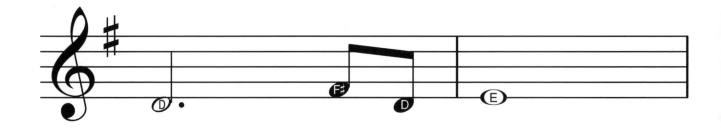

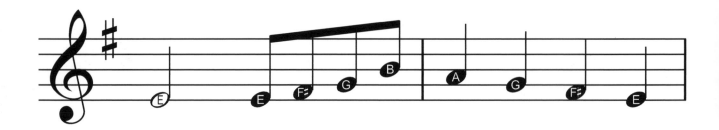

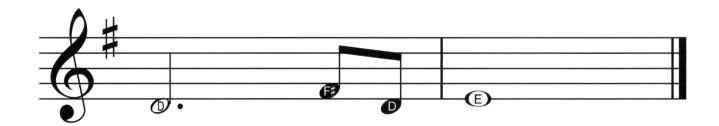

Baa Baa Black Sheep

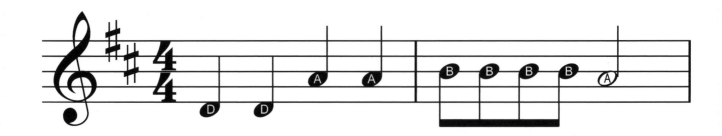

Fine

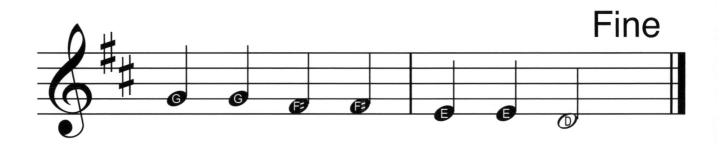

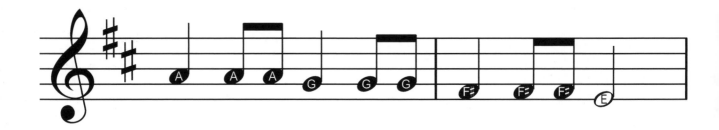

D.C. al Coda

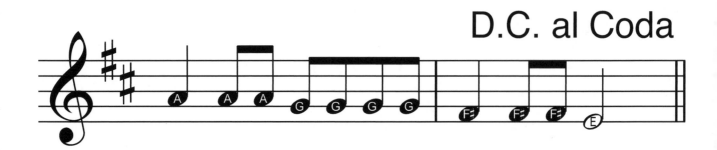

Brahms symphony

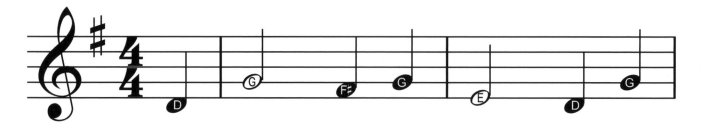

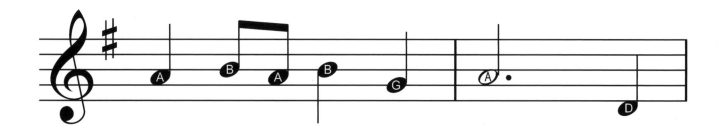

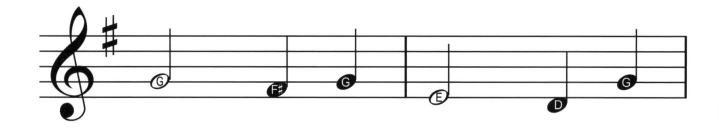

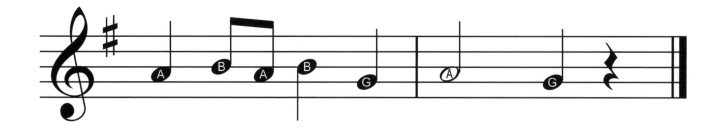

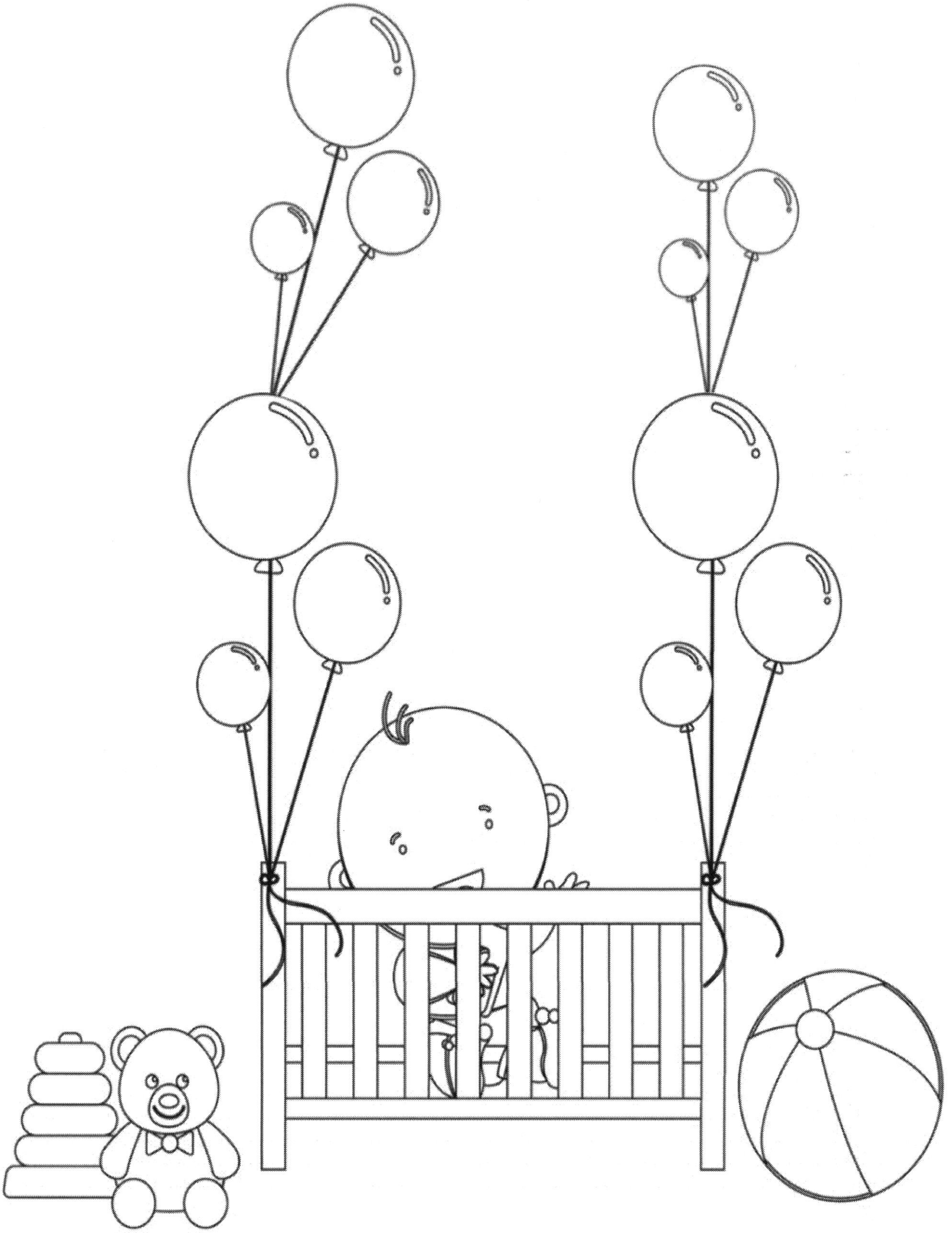

This Little Light of Mine

Up on the House Top

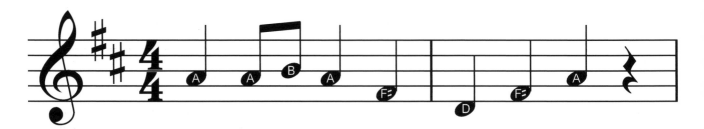

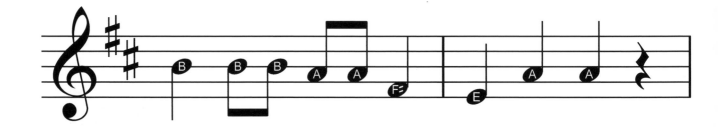

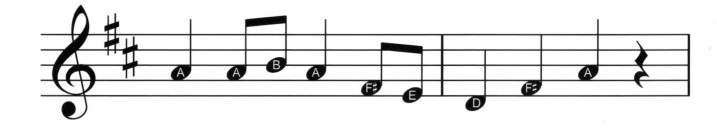

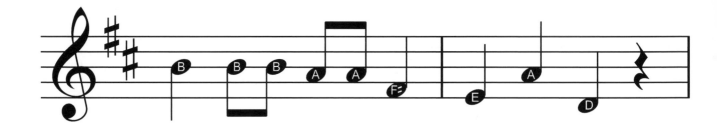

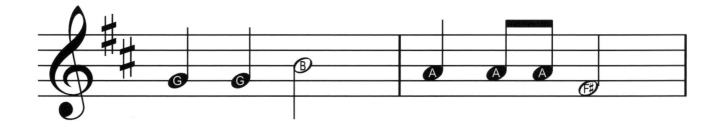

This Old Man

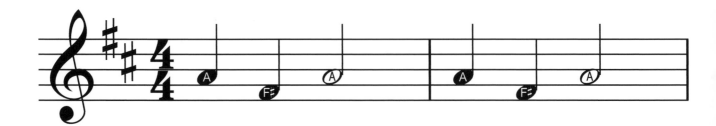

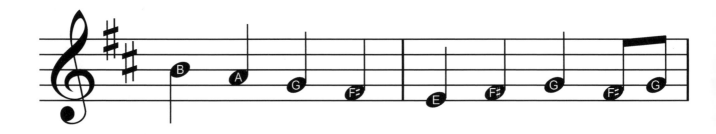

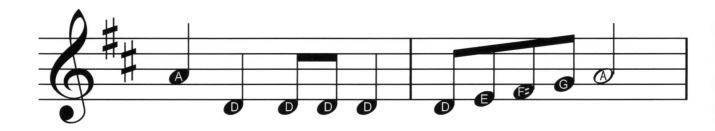

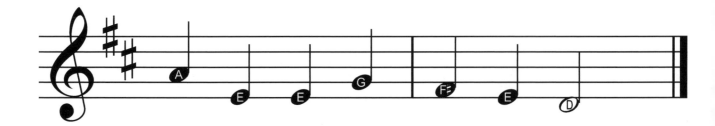

Old MacDonald

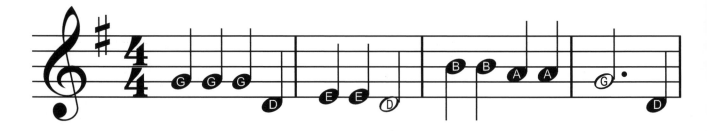

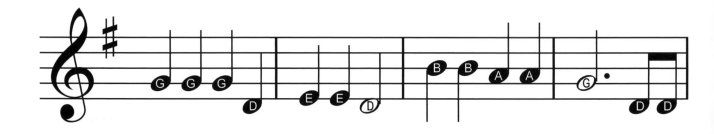

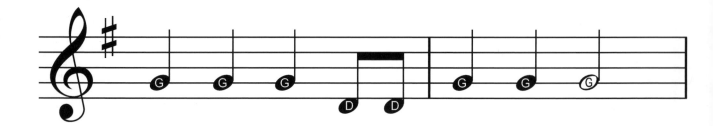

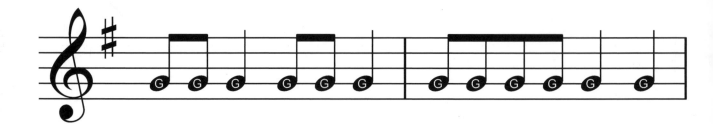

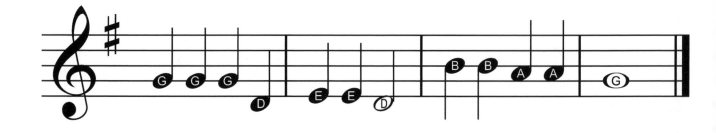

Spring Theme

ROCK·a·my·soul

Largo

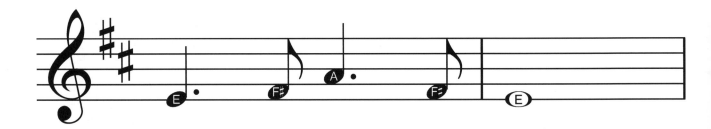

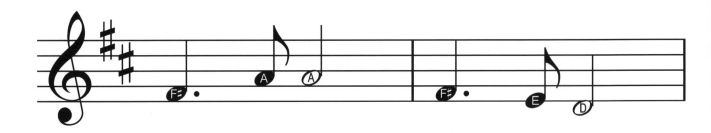

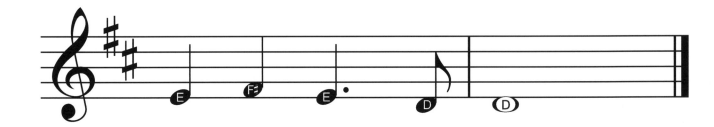

Kum Ba Yah

Ode to Joy

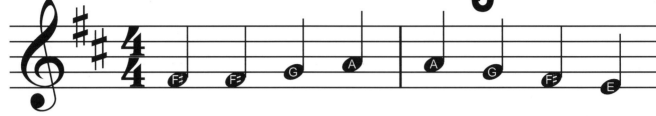

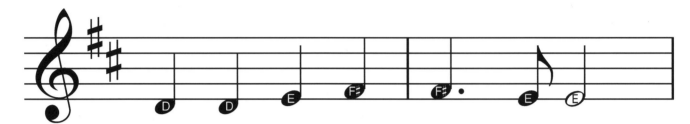

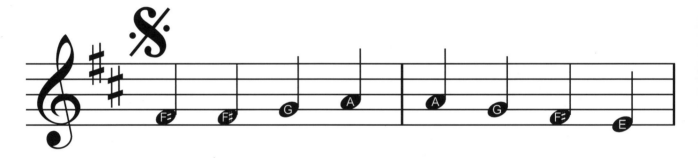

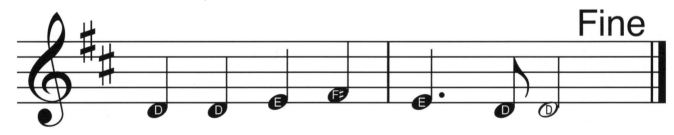

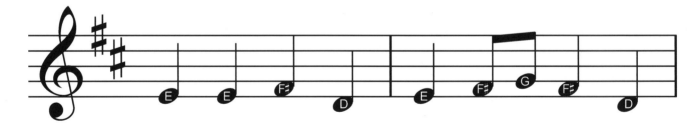

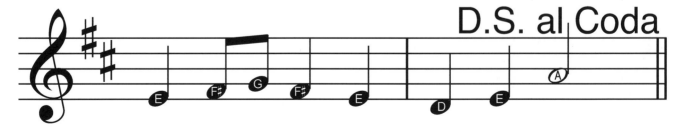

Oh, Susana

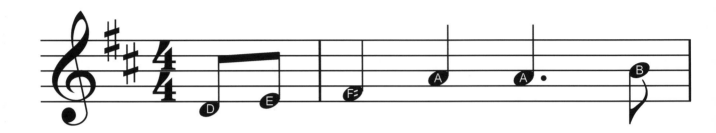

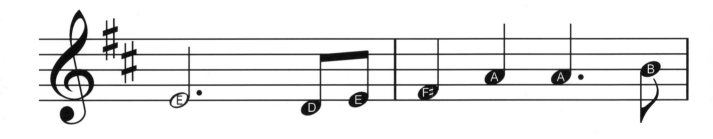

shepherd's Hey

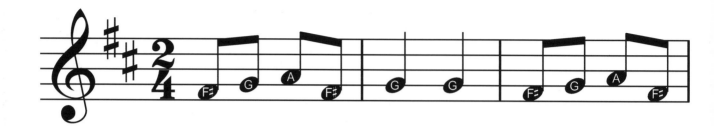

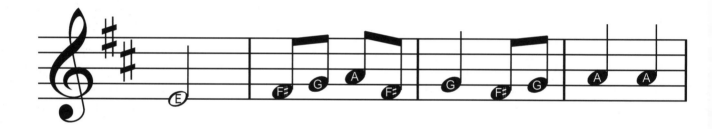

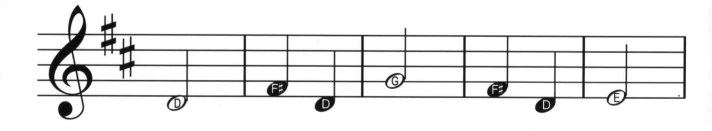

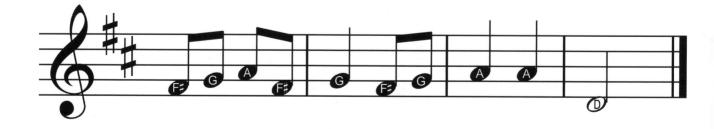

Hot Cross Buns

Good King Wenceslas

Mary Had a Little Lamb

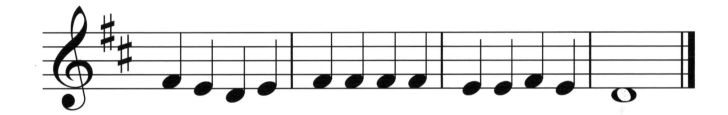

Lightly Row

Aura Lee

Go Tell Aunt Rhody

Frog Song

Camptown Races

68

London Bridge

Dreydl, Dreydl

Twinkle, Twinkle, Little Star

Jolly Old St. Nicholas

The Bridge at Avignon

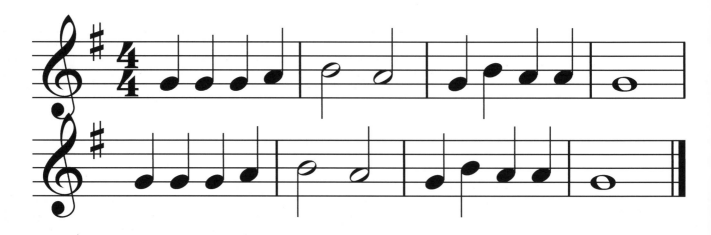

Pop Goes the Weasel

Jingle Bells

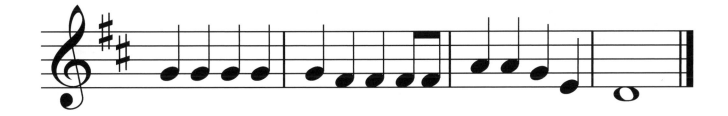

Are You sleeping?

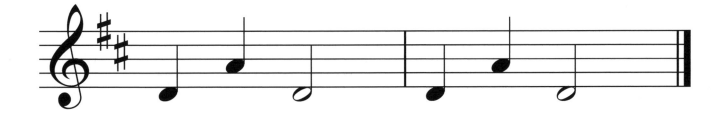

Musette

Lo Yisa Goy

Baa Baa Black sheep

Fine

D.C. al Coda

Brahms symphony

This Little Light of Mine

Up on the House Top

This Old Man

Old MacDonald

Spring Theme

Rock-a-my-soul

Largo

Kum Ba Yah

Ode to Joy

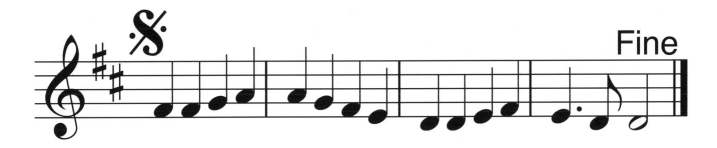

oh, susana

shepherd's Hey